How to Use the Activity Centers

Special One-Day Experience

Set aside a block of two to four hours on one day for students to move through the centers for a season. This gives the day a special feeling and formally salutes the season.

Throughout the Season

Use the centers over a period of time during the appropriate season. Set up one or more center for a specific number of days, organizing a schedule for students to follow. Change the center(s) when all students have completed that task.

Skills Practiced

Skills being practiced are listed on the introductory page for each season and on the teacher-direction page for the specific center. Students will practice the following skills:

- Classifying
- Sorting
- Patterning
- Generalizing
- Comparing and Contrasting
- Mental Imagery

- Fluency
- Deductive Reasoning
- Observing
- Divergent Thinking
- Ordering
- Following Directions

In addition, students will experience working independently or with a partner. The hands-on approach in a nonthreatening environment helps to build confidence and the willingness to be a risk-taker.

Helpful Hints

One-Day Approach

- Prepare in advance the materials for all centers you plan to use.
- Call in parents and other volunteers to help for the day.
- Make a booklet for each student containing all the needed center information and record sheets.
- Make sure students have worked on the skill being presented in the center. This should not be the first time a child sees a concept.
- Before students begin, introduce each center, walking students through what will be expected. Have them go through their student booklets at the same time.
- Encourage students to help one another at a center before asking for adult help.
- Traveling Rules—Set a timer to indicate when students can move to a new center.

Independent Center Approach

- Prepare in advance the materials for centers you intend to use.
- Make student booklets containing only the materials needed for the centers you plan to set up.
- Introduce each center before you let students work with it.
- Let at least two students work at each center. They can provide help for each other, minimizing the need for teacher help.

Follow-Up

Build in time for closure once the centers are completed. This is an integral part of the experience. Comparing results brings out additional points of view, new strategies, and reinforces the fact that there can be more than one correct answer in many situations.

Be Prepared

Have an extra activity available for students who finish early. The coloring activity at the beginning of each section may be used for this purpose.

Contents

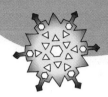

About the Activity Centers

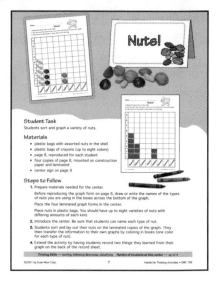

Teacher Page

- The thinking skills practiced by the activity and the number of students who may work at the center
- A description of the student's task
- A list of materials
- Steps to follow

Record Forms

Reproducible forms for students to complete at the center

Full-Color Cutouts

Ready-to-use color center signs and display items

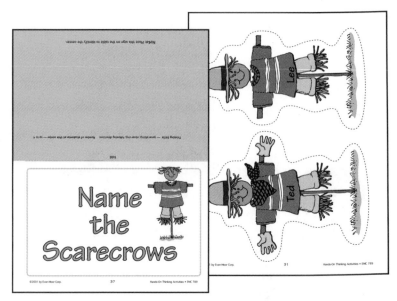

Autumn Activity Centers

Thinking Skills Assessed

Name of Center	Following Directions	Classifying	Sorting	Observing	Generalizing	Ordering	Divergent Thinking	Comparing/ Contrasting	Fluency	Deductive Reasoning	Mental Imagery
Nuts!	🍁	🍁	🍁								
An Apple	🍁			🍁							
Kites	🍁	🍁				🍁					
Pumpkins	🍁										
Name the Scarecrows	🍁			🍁	🍁						
Larry's Leaves	🍁				🍁	🍁		🍁			
Seeds to Pumpkins	🍁										
Who Likes Pumpkin Pie?	🍁						🍁			🍁	
Picking Apples	🍁								🍁		

Name _____

Autumn

Color the leaves.

Make each set of leaves different in one way.

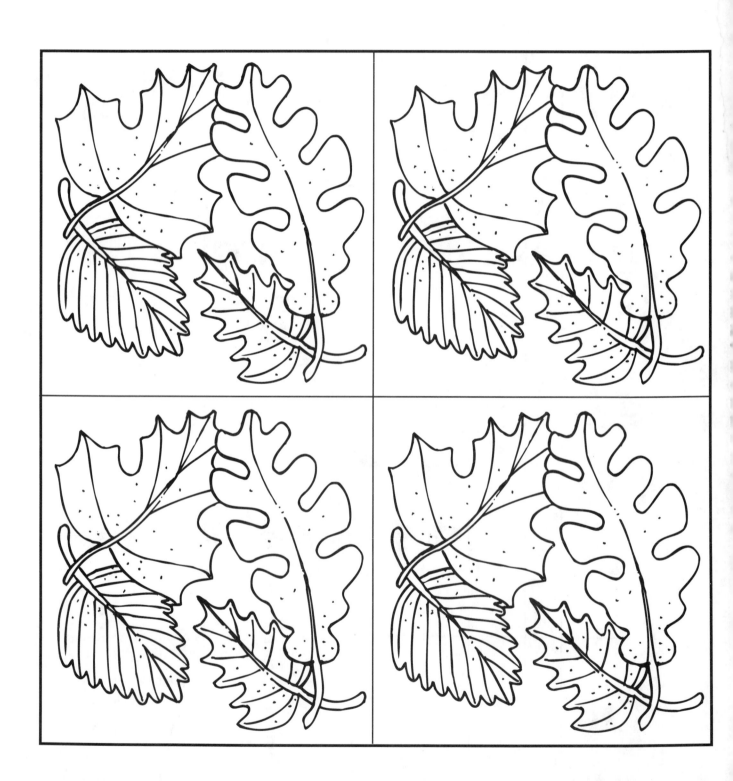

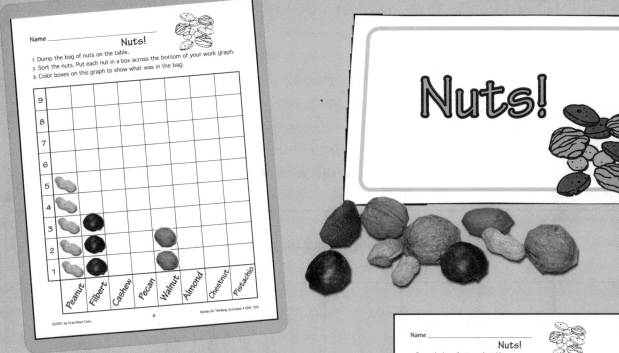

Student Task

Students sort and graph a variety of nuts.

Materials

- plastic bags with assorted nuts in the shell
- plastic bags of crayons (up to eight colors)
- page 8, reproduced for each student
- four copies of page 8, mounted on construction paper and laminated
- center sign on page 9

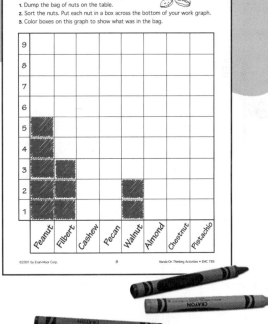

Steps to Follow

1. Prepare materials needed for the center.

   Before reproducing the graph form on page 8, draw or write the names of the types of nuts you are using in the boxes across the bottom of the graph.

   Place the four laminated graph forms in the center.

   Place nuts in plastic bags. You should have up to eight varieties of nuts with differing amounts of each kind.

2. Introduce the center. Be sure that students can name each type of nut.

3. Students sort and lay out their nuts on the laminated copies of the graph. They then transfer the information to their own graphs by coloring in boxes (one color for each type of nut).

4. Extend the activity by having students record two things they learned from their graph on the back of the record sheet.

Thinking Skills — sorting; following directions; classifying   **Number of students at this center** — up to 4

©2001 by Evan-Moor Corp.   7   Hands-On Thinking Activities • EMC 789

Name _____

Nuts!

1. Dump the bag of nuts on the table.
2. Sort the nuts. Put each nut in a box across the bottom of your work graph.
3. Color boxes on this graph to show what was in the bag.

9								
8								
7								
6								
5								
4								
3								
2								
1								

Note: Place this sign on the table to identify the center.

Thinking Skills — sorting; following directions; classifying   **Number of students at this center** — up to 4

fold

Nuts!

Note: Place this sign on the table to identify the center.

9   Hands-On Thinking Activities • EMC 789

red
green
shiny
crunchy
sweet
smooth

An Apple— Using My Five Senses

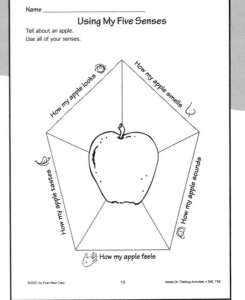

Name _____

Using My Five Senses

Tell about an apple.
Use all of your senses.

How my apple looks

How my apple smells

How my apple tastes

How my apple sounds

How my apple feels

©2001 by Evan-Moor Corp.   12   Hands-On Thinking Activities • EMC 789

Student Task

Students experience an apple with all their senses. They write words or phrases on a record sheet to describe what they sense.

Materials

- small apples cut into wedges
- small paper plates
- pencils or crayons
- chart paper
- page 12, reproduced for each student
- center sign on page 13

Steps to Follow

1. Prepare materials needed for the center.

   At the beginning of each center session, slice apples into wedges and place them on small paper plates. Use several kinds of apples to encourage more variety in the students' descriptions.

2. Introduce the center. Brainstorm a list of words that describe how things taste, sound, feel, smell, and look. Write these words on a chart to serve as a word bank at the center. (This chart can be used again with the "Five Senses" activities for winter, spring, and summer.)

3. Encourage students at the center to talk about what they discover as they taste, feel, etc., their apple wedges. Then they write descriptive words in each section of the worksheet.

Thinking Skills — observing; following directions   **Number of students at this center** — up to 4

Name _____

Using My Five Senses

Tell about an apple.
Use all of your senses.

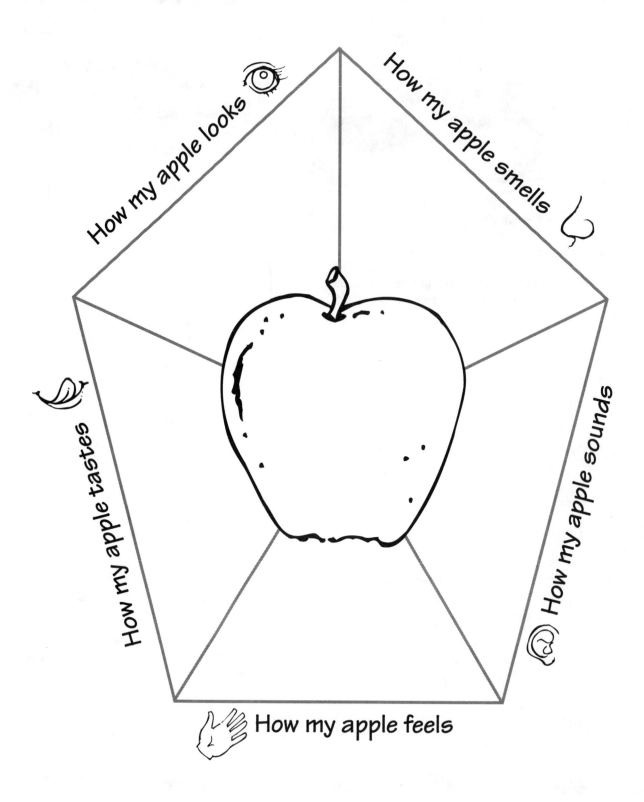

Thinking Skills — observing; following directions   Number of students at this center — up to 4

fold

An Apple—
Using My Five Senses

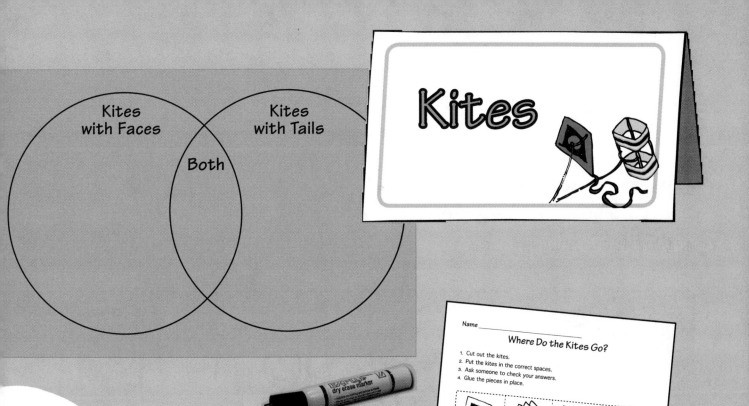

Student Task

Students categorize kites on a Venn diagram.

Materials

- 12″ x 18″ (30.5 x 45.5 cm) construction paper, one per student
- black marking pen
- scissors and glue
- page 16, reproduced for each student
- center sign on page 17

Steps to Follow

1. Prepare materials needed for the center.

Make a Venn diagram for each student by drawing large circles on the construction paper sheets. Label the spaces as shown. (This is a great job for parent volunteers.)

2. Introduce the center by reviewing how to use a Venn diagram. Be sure students are clear about the attributes they are looking for.

3. Students cut out the kites, sort them, and place them on the Venn diagram in the correct categories.

Have students ask someone to check their answers before gluing down the kites.

4. Extend the activity for more able students by asking them to list other attributes of the kites on the back of their diagram sheets.

Thinking Skills — classifying; ordering; following directions   **Number of students at this center** — up to 4

Where Do the Kites Go?

1. Cut out the kites.
2. Put the kites in the correct spaces.
3. Ask someone to check your answers.
4. Glue the pieces in place.

Thinking Skills — classifying; ordering; following directions   Number of students at this center — up to 4

fold

Kites

Hands-On Thinking Activities • EMC 789

Student Task

Students complete checklists as they examine two pumpkins.

Materials

- a large real pumpkin
- a small artificial pumpkin
- page 20, reproduced for each student
- center sign on page 21

Steps to Follow

1. Prepare materials needed for the center.

   Place a label beside each pumpkin. Label the real pumpkin "A" and the artificial pumpkin "B."

2. Discuss with students how they can share the two pumpkins while they are working at the center. *(Two people can use one pumpkin at the same time. We can take turns. We can help each other find the answers.)*

3. Introduce the center. Ask students to identify the parts asked for on the record sheet (stem, leaves, stripes). Review what they are to record on the record sheet.

Thinking Skills — comparing and contrasting; following directions   **Number of students at this center** — up to 4

Name _____

Pumpkins

Look at the two pumpkins.

	Pumpkin A	Pumpkin B
How many stripes?		
How many stems?		
How many leaves?		

Write 2 ways the pumpkins are alike.

_____

_____

Write 2 ways the pumpkins are different.

_____

_____

Draw pumpkin A.	Draw pumpkin B.

Note: Place this sign on the table to identify the center.

Thinking Skills — comparing and contrasting; following directions   Number of students at this center — up to 4

fold

Pumpkins

Note: Place this sign on the table to identify the center.

Hands-On Thinking Activities • EMC 789

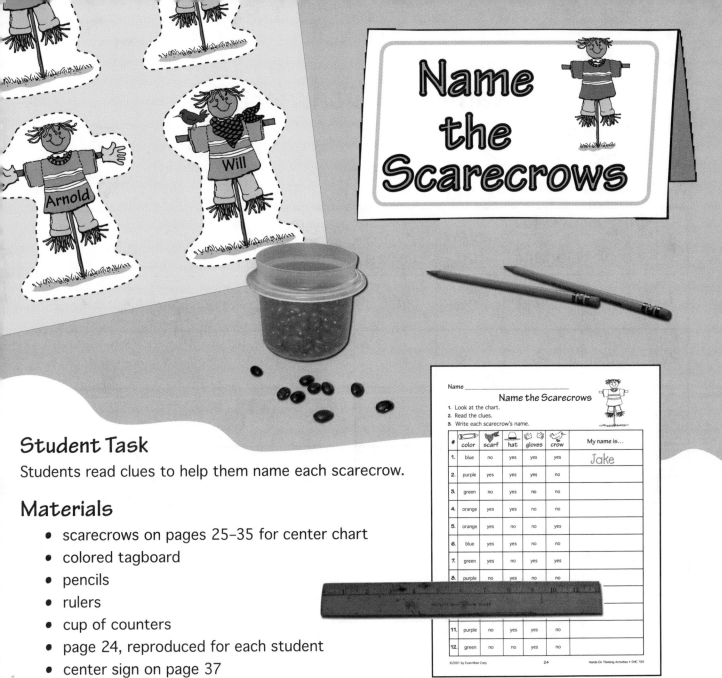

Student Task

Students read clues to help them name each scarecrow.

Materials

- scarecrows on pages 25–35 for center chart
- colored tagboard
- pencils
- rulers
- cup of counters
- page 24, reproduced for each student
- center sign on page 37

Steps to Follow

1. Prepare materials needed for the center.

Glue the scarecrows on pages 25–35 to a sheet of colored tagboard. Place the chart on the center table.

2. Students use the clues on the record sheet to identify each scarecrow. They write the scarecrow's name on the record sheet.

Demonstrate how to use a ruler placed under each line of clues to help students keep their place as they read the clues.

Students can place a counter on each scarecrow on the chart as it is identified.

3. Extend the activity by asking students to draw a scarecrow on the back of their record sheets and then write clues describing it.

Thinking Skills — generalizing; observing; following directions   **Number of students at this center** — up to 4

Name _____

Name the Scarecrows

1. Look at the chart.
2. Read the clues.
3. Write each scarecrow's name.

#	color	scarf	hat	gloves	crow	My name is…
1.	blue	no	yes	yes	yes	Jake
2.	purple	yes	yes	yes	no	
3.	green	no	yes	no	no	
4.	orange	yes	yes	no	no	
5.	orange	yes	no	no	yes	
6.	blue	yes	yes	no	no	
7.	green	yes	no	yes	yes	
8.	purple	no	yes	no	no	
9.	blue	no	no	yes	yes	
10.	orange	no	no	yes	no	
11.	purple	no	yes	yes	no	
12.	green	no	no	yes	no	

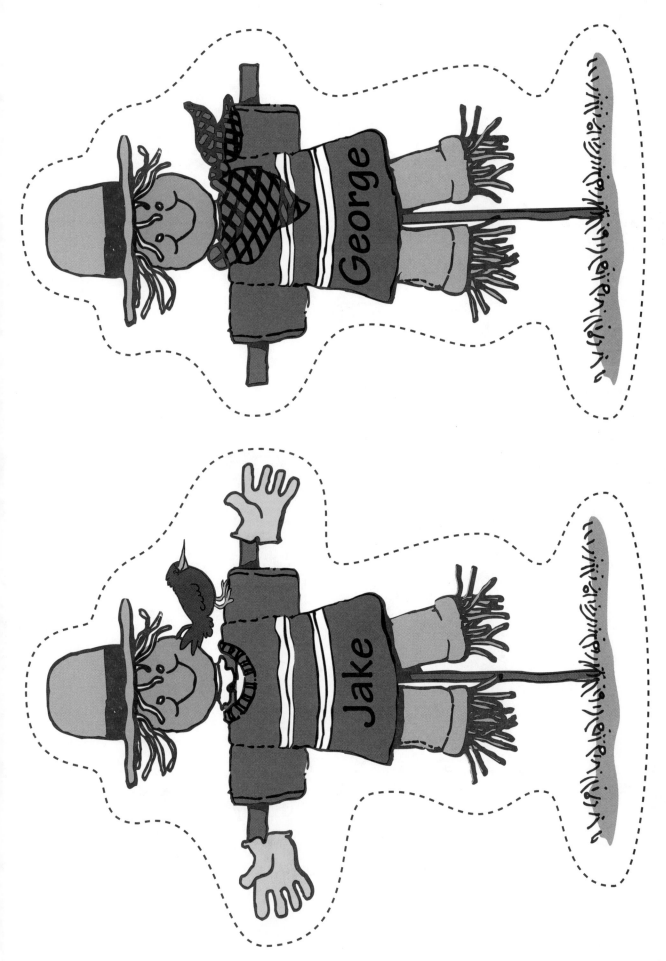

27

Hands-On Thinking Activities • EMC 789

29

Hands-On Thinking Activities • EMC 789

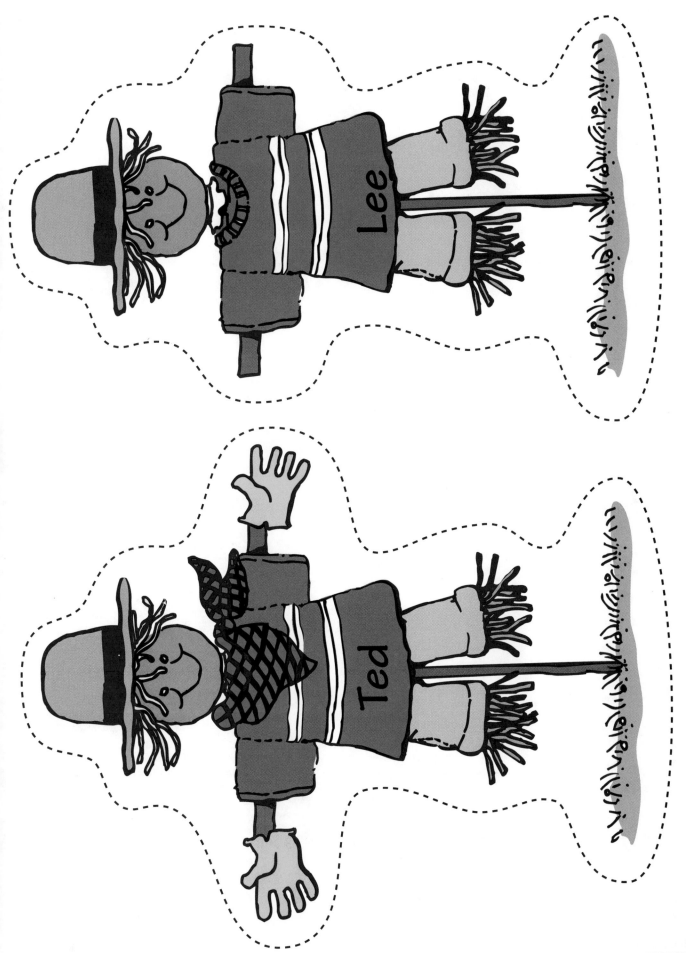

31

Hands-On Thinking Activities • EMC 789

Hands-On Thinking Activities • EMC 789

Hands-On Thinking Activities • EMC 789

Hands-On Thinking Activities • EMC 789

Thinking Skills — generalizing; observing; following directions   Number of students at this center — up to 4

fold

Name the Scarecrows

Hands-On Thinking Activities • EMC 789

Hands-On Thinking Activities • EMC 789

Student Task

Students generalize what characteristic is common to a set of leaves.

Materials

- pencils
- page 40, reproduced for each student
- center sign on page 41

Steps to Follow

1. Prepare materials needed for the center.

2. Review ways to solve this type of puzzle. Remind students to look carefully at the pictures and to ask themselves questions such as, "What is the same about the pictures in row one? How are the pictures in row one different?"

3. Students locate one common characteristic among the items in the first row that is missing in the items in the second row. They then mark any leaves in the final row that can be part of Larry's collection.

4. Extend the activity by having students turn their papers over and draw another leaf that could be part of Larry's collection.

Thinking Skills — generalizing; following directions   **Number of students at this center** — up to 4

Name_____

Larry's Leaves

Help Larry pick leaves for his collection.
These are Larry's leaves.

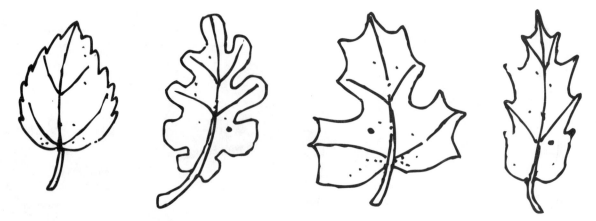

These are not Larry's leaves.

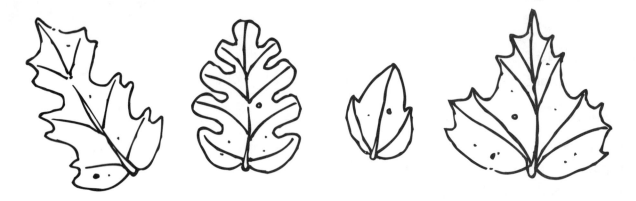

Mark the leaves that Larry would pick for his collection.

What did all of Larry's leaves have?

_____

     Hands-On Thinking Activities • EMC 789

Thinking Skills — generalizing; following directions   Number of students at this center — up to 4

fold

Larry's Leaves

Note: Place this sign on the table to identify the center.

41

Hands-On Thinking Activities • EMC 789

Student Task

Students place the steps of a pumpkin's life cycle in order. Then they draw a picture to show how they would use the mature pumpkin.

Materials

- 4″ x 18″ (10 x 45.5 cm) construction paper strips, one per student
- writing paper
- scissors and glue
- page 44, reproduced for each student
- center sign on page 45

Steps to Follow

1. Prepare materials for the center. You will need one construction paper strip for each student.

2. Introduce the center. Explain to students that they are to cut the pictures apart and then paste them in order on their construction paper strip. Remind them to start with the seed on the left side of the strip. In the blank box, they are to draw a picture showing what they would do with the ripe pumpkin. This will be the last picture in the sequence.

3. Extend the activity by asking students to write about each step on a sheet of writing paper.

Thinking Skills — ordering; following directions   **Number of students at this center** — up to 4

Name _____

Seeds to Pumpkins

Cut the pictures apart. Paste them in order on your paper strip.

What you would do with your pumpkin?

Thinking Skills — ordering; following directions   **Number of students at this center** — up to 4

fold

Seeds
to
Pumpkins

Who Likes Pumpkin Pie?

Name _____

Who Likes Pumpkin Pie?

Use the clues to find out what each child had for a snack.
Color the correct boxes.

1. Tomas put salt on his snack.
2. Ann held a cone to eat her snack.
3. Bill and Kim ate their snacks with a fork.
4. Bill doesn't like cake.

	pumpkin pie	ice cream	popcorn	cake
Ann				
Bill				
Kim				
Tomas				

Turn this paper over. Draw a snack you like to eat. Tell why you like it.

©2001 by Evan-Moor Corp.   48   Hands-On Thinking Activities • EMC 789

Student Task

Students use clues to figure out which person likes pumpkin pie.

Materials

- container of counters
- crayons
- page 48, reproduced for each student
- center sign on page 49

Steps to Follow

1. Prepare materials for the center.

2. Discuss strategies for working a logic matrix. Read the clues and put a counter on the correct box. If there can be no other answer for that person, make an X in all the other boxes after that name. Since each person eats only one thing, make an X on all the other boxes under that food. For example: Make an X on all the other foods in Ann's row. Also make an X on all the other boxes under ice cream.

   Explain to students that once they are happy with their answers, they are to remove the counters one at a time, coloring in the boxes they have marked.

   If students have had limited experience solving a matrix problem, have them work in pairs.

Thinking Skills — deductive reasoning; following directions   **Number of students at this center** — up to 4

Name _____

Who Likes Pumpkin Pie?

Use the clues to find out what each child had for a snack.
Color the correct boxes.

1. Tomas put salt on his snack.
2. Ann held a cone to eat her snack.
3. Bill and Kim ate their snacks with a fork.
4. Bill doesn't like cake.

	pumpkin pie	ice cream	popcorn	cake
Ann				
Bill				
Kim				
Tomas				

Turn this paper over. Draw a snack you like to eat. Tell why you like it.

Thinking Skills — deductive reasoning; following directions   Number of students at this center — up to 4

fold

Who Likes Pumpkin Pie?

Hands-On Thinking Activities • EMC 789

Student Task

Students think of various ways to get an apple down from a tree.

Materials

- writing paper
- pencils
- page 52, reproduced for each student
- center sign on page 53

Steps to Follow

1. Prepare materials needed for the center.

2. Students think of six ways Jo Jo can pick the big apple in the tree. They may draw or write their suggestions.

3. They then select one picking method and explain how that method could also be used to rescue a cat caught in a tree.

Thinking Skills — divergent thinking; fluency; following directions   **Number of students at this center** — up to 4

Name _____

Picking Apples

Jo Jo wants the big red apple in this tree.
Write or draw six ways he can get the apple.

1.	**2.**
3.	**4.**
5.	**6.**

Pick the way you would use to
get this kitten out of the tree.

Tell why you picked this way.

Hands-On Thinking Activities • EMC 789

Note: Place this sign on the table to identify the center.

Thinking Skills — divergent thinking; fluency; following directions

Number of students at this center — up to 4

fold

Picking Apples

Winter Activity Centers

Thinking Skills Assessed

Name of Center	Following Directions	Classifying	Sorting	Observing	Generalizing	Ordering	Divergent Thinking	Comparing/ Contrasting	Fluency	Deductive Reasoning	Mental Imagery
Ice-Skating	❄										❄
Winter Hats	❄	❄	❄								
A Cookie	❄			❄							
Polar Bears	❄							❄			
Gingerbread Men	❄					❄					
A Herd of Reindeer	❄				❄						
Who Likes Hot Chocolate?	❄						❄			❄	
Building a Snowman	❄					❄			❄		
Name the Snowmen	❄	❄		❄							

Name _____

Winter

Color the snowflakes.

Make each snowflake different in one way.

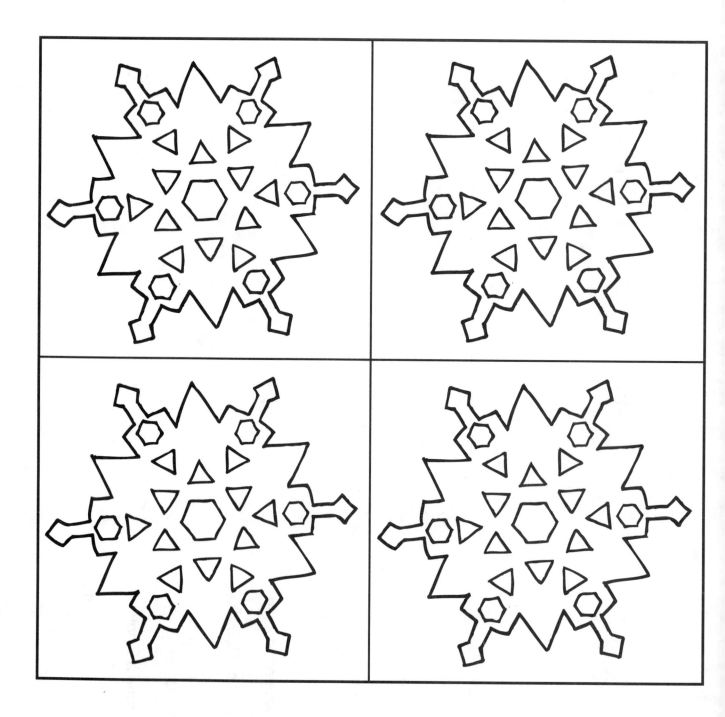

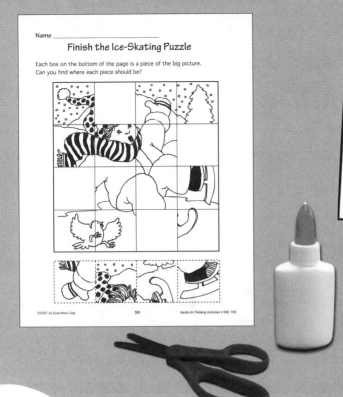

Name
Finish the Ice-Skating Puzzle

Each box on the bottom of the page is a piece of the big picture.
Can you find where each piece should be?

©2001 by Evan-Moor Corp.   58   Hands-On Thinking Activities • EMC 789

Name
Look at the clues.   What Is It?
Draw the rest of the picture.
It is a _____

©2001 by Evan-Moor Corp.   61   Hands-On Thinking Activities • EMC 789

Student Task

Students visualize the relationship of a part to the whole.

Materials

- scissors and glue
- crayons
- pages 58 and 61, reproduced for each student
- center sign on page 59

Steps to Follow

1. Prepare materials needed for the center.

2. Encourage students to work together and describe the small pieces to each other. (*This piece looks like part of an ice skate. I think this is part of the skater's arm.*)

3. Students complete two tasks.

   - On the first form, they determine where each small puzzle part fits in the picture. They then paste the small piece in the correct place on the large picture.
   - On the second form, they use the visual clues to help them draw the missing parts of an object related to their other puzzle.

Thinking Skills — mental imagery; following directions   **Number of students at this center** — up to 4

Finish the Ice-Skating Puzzle

Each box on the bottom of the page is a piece of the big picture. Can you find where each piece should be?

Thinking Skills — mental imagery; following directions   Number of students at this center — up to 4

fold

Ice-Skating—
Finish the Puzzle

Hands-On Thinking Activities • EMC 789

Name _____

What Is It?

Look at the clues.

Draw the rest of the picture.

It is a _____ .

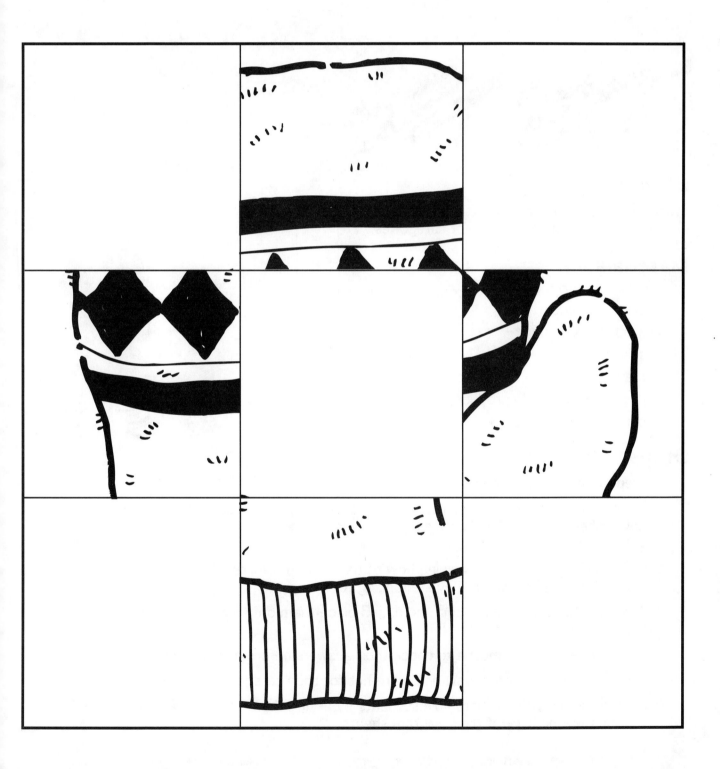

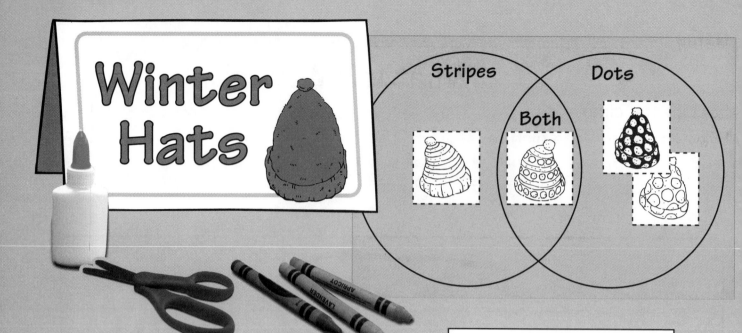

Winter Hats

Stripes   Both   Dots

Student Task

Students cut out the hats, sort them, and place them on the Venn diagram in the correct categories.

Materials

- 12″ x 18″ (30.5 x 45.5 cm) construction paper, one per student
- black marking pen
- scissors and glue
- crayons
- pages 63 and 64, reproduced for each student
- center sign on page 65

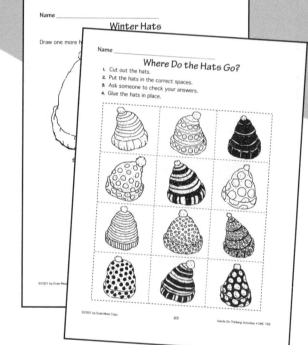

Steps to Follow

1. Prepare materials needed for the center.

   Make a Venn diagram for each student by drawing large circles on the construction paper sheets. Label the spaces as shown below. (This is a great job for parent volunteers.)

2. Introduce the center by reviewing how to use a Venn diagram. Be sure students are clear about the attributes they are looking for.

3. Students cut out the hats, sort them, and place them on the Venn diagram in the correct categories.

   Have students ask someone to check their answers before gluing down the hats.

4. Using page 64, students draw one more hat for each category.

5. Extend the activity for more able students by asking them to list other attributes of the hats on the back of their diagram sheets.

Thinking Skills — classifying; sorting; following directions   **Number of students at this center** — up to 4

Name _____

Where Do the Hats Go?

1. Cut out the hats.
2. Put the hats in the correct spaces.
3. Ask someone to check your answers.
4. Glue the hats in place.

Hands-On Thinking Activities • EMC 789

Winter Hats

Draw one more hat that would go in each space.

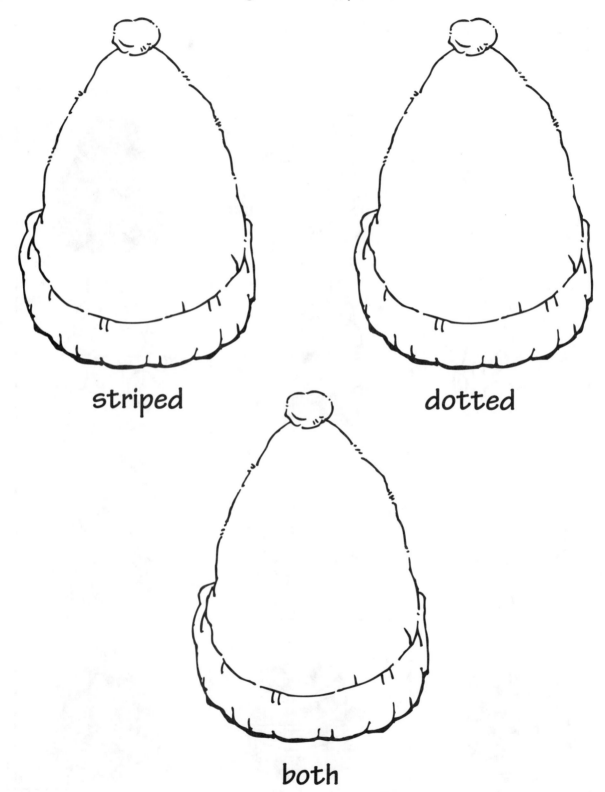

striped

dotted

both

fold

Winter Hats

Hands-On Thinking Activities • EMC 789

soft   rough
hard   round
crunchy   brown
spicy   pink
lumpy   white

A Cookie—
Using My Five Senses

Student Task

Students experience a cookie with all of their senses. They write words or phrases on a record sheet to describe what they sense.

Materials

- cookies, three different kinds
- small paper plates
- pencils or crayons
- chart paper
- page 68, reproduced for each student
- center sign on page 69

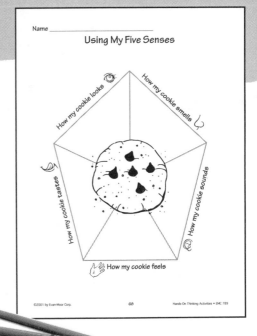

Name _____

Using My Five Senses

How my cookie looks / How my cookie smells / How my cookie tastes / How my cookie sounds / How my cookie feels

©2001 by Evan-Moor Corp.   68   Hands-On Thinking Activities • EMC 789

Steps to Follow

1. Prepare materials needed for the center.

   At the beginning of each center session, place one of each type of cookie on small paper plates for the students to observe.

2. Introduce the center. Brainstorm a list of words that describe how things taste, sound, feel, smell, and look. Write these words on a chart to serve as a word bank at the center. (Or use the chart started on page 11.)

3. Encourage students at the center to talk about what they discover as they taste, feel, etc., their cookies. Then they write descriptive words in each section of the worksheet.

Thinking Skills — observing; following directions   *Number of students at this center* — up to 4

Name _____

Using My Five Senses

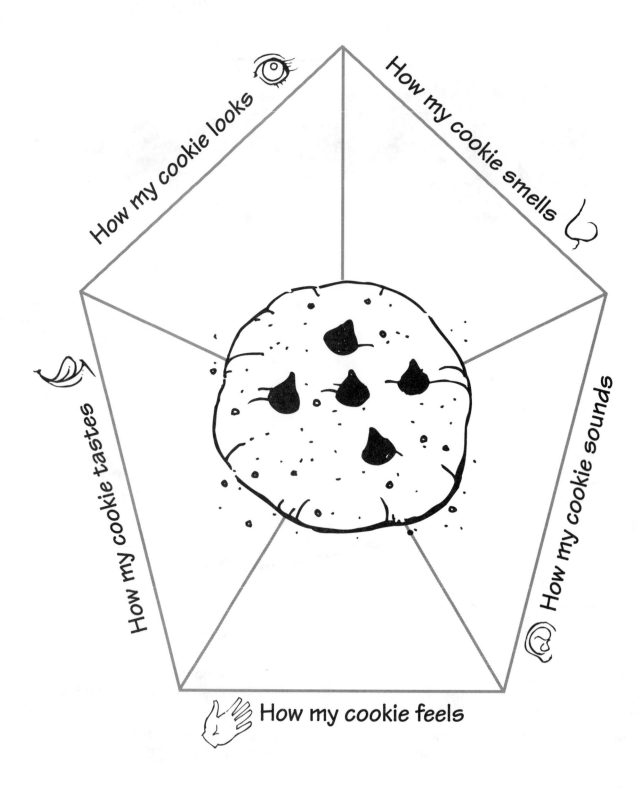

How my cookie looks

How my cookie smells

How my cookie tastes

How my cookie sounds

How my cookie feels

Hands-On Thinking Activities • EMC 789

fold

Thinking Skills — observing; following directions   **Number of students at this center** — up to 4

A Cookie—
Using My
Five Senses

Student Task

Students look for similarities and differences as they compare pictures of polar bears.

Materials

- pencils
- page 72, reproduced for each student
- center sign on page 73

Steps to Follow

1. Prepare the materials needed for the center.

2. Students look at each polar bear to determine how the bears are alike and how they are different. They then mark the two bears that are identical.

3. Encourage students at the center to discuss the similarities and differences they see as they examine the bears.

4. Extend the activity by asking students to list two or more ways the bears were alike on the back of their worksheets.

Thinking Skills — comparing and contrasting; following directions   **Number of students at this center** — up to 4

Name _____

Polar Bears

Look at the polar bears.
How are they alike?
How are they different?

Mark the two bears that are just alike.

Thinking Skills — comparing and contrasting; following directions   **Number of students at this center** — up to 4

fold

Polar Bears

Hands-On Thinking Activities • EMC 789

Gingerbread Men

Student Task

Students place in order the steps for making gingerbread men cookies.

Materials

- 4″ x 18″ (10 x 45.5 cm) construction paper strips, one per student
- writing paper
- scissors and glue
- pencils and crayons
- page 76, reproduced for each student
- center sign on page 77

Steps to Follow

1. Prepare materials needed for the center.

2. Introduce the center. Explain to students that they are to cut the pieces apart and then paste them in order on their construction paper strip. Remind them to start with the bowl and ingredients on the left side of the strip. In the blank box, they are to draw a picture showing what part of the gingerbread cookie they would eat first. This will be the last picture in the sequence.

3. Extend the activity by asking students to write about each step on a sheet of writing paper.

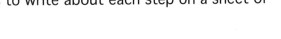

Thinking Skills — ordering; following directions   **Number of students at this center** — up to 4

Name _____

Making Gingerbread Men

Cut the pictures apart. Paste them in order.

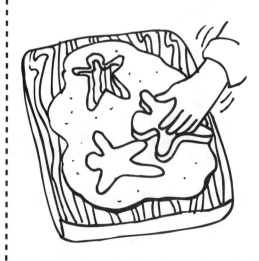

What part of the cookie would you eat first?

Thinking Skills — ordering; following directions   **Number of students at this center** — up to 4

fold

Gingerbread Men

Students Task

Students generalize what characteristics are common to a set of reindeer.

Materials

- pencils
- crayons
- page 80, reproduced for each student
- center sign on page 81

Steps to Follow

1. Prepare materials needed for the center.

2. Review ways to solve this type of puzzle. Remind students to look carefully at the pictures and to ask themselves questions such as, "What is the same about the pictures in row one? How are the pictures in row one different?"

3. Students locate two characteristics common to the reindeer in the first row that are missing in the reindeer in the second row. They then add details to the final reindeer to make it part of the herd.

4. Extend the activity by having students explain how they decided which reindeer was a part of the herd.

Thinking Skills — generalizing; following directions   **Number of students at this center** — up to 4

A Herd of Reindeer

Reindeer live in herds.

These reindeer are a part of a herd.

These reindeer are not a part of the herd.

Make this reindeer a part of the herd.

What rule did you follow?

_____

_____

Thinking Skills — generalizing; following directions   Number of students at this center — up to 4

fold

A Herd of Reindeer

81

Hands-On Thinking Activities • EMC 789

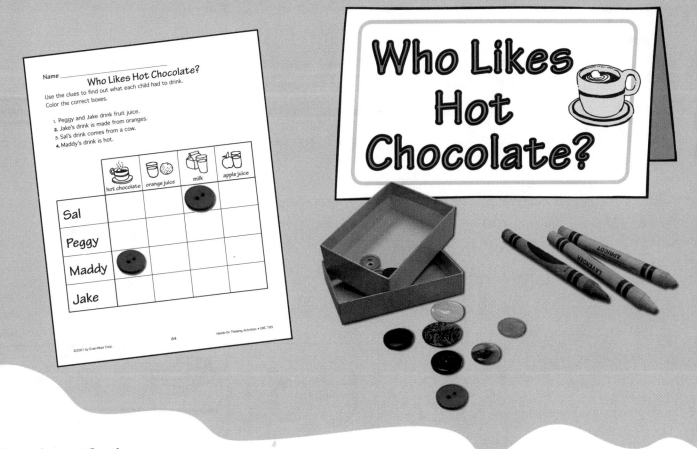

Student Task

Students use clues to figure out which person likes hot chocolate.

Materials

- container of counters
- crayons
- page 84, reproduced for each student
- center sign on page 85

Steps to Follow

1. Prepare materials for the center.

2. Discuss strategies for working a logic matrix. Read the clues and put a counter on the correct box. If there can be no other answer for that person, make an X in all the other boxes after that name. Since each person drinks only one thing, make an X on all the other boxes under that drink. For example: Jake's drink is made from oranges, so put a counter on orange juice in Jake's row. Make an X on all the other drinks in Jake's row. Also make an X on all the other boxes under orange juice.

   Explain to students that once they are happy with their answers, they are to remove the counters one at a time, coloring in the boxes they have marked.

   If students have had limited experience solving a matrix problem, have them work in pairs.

Thinking Skills — deductive reasoning; following directions   **Number of students at this center** — up to 4

Name _____

Who Likes Hot Chocolate?

Use the clues to find out what each child had to drink.
Color the correct boxes.

1. Peggy and Jake drink fruit juice.
2. Jake's drink is made from oranges.
3. Sal's drink comes from a cow.
4. Maddy's drink is hot.

	hot chocolate	orange juice	milk	apple juice
Sal				
Peggy				
Maddy				
Jake				

 Hands-On Thinking Activities • EMC 789

Thinking Skills — deductive reasoning; following directions

Number of students at this center — up to 4

fold

Who Likes Hot Chocolate?

85

Hands-On Thinking Activities • EMC 789

Hands-On Thinking Activities • EMC 789

a snow
puppy
with
a bowl of
pebbles
for bones

a whole
snow
people
family

Building a Snowman

fat
snow lady
wearing a
funny hat

a snow
dinosaur

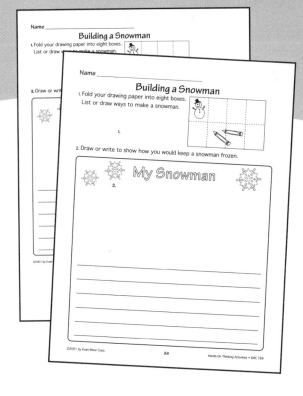

Student Task

Students think of various kinds of snowmen they could build. They then think of a way to keep a snowman from melting.

Materials

- pencils
- drawing paper
- page 88, reproduced for each student
- center sign on page 89

Steps to Follow

1. Prepare materials needed for the center.

2. Introduce the center. Show students how to fold drawing paper into eight boxes. Students list or draw up to eight different kinds of snowmen they could build.

3. Students choose one of their snowmen and describe a way to keep it from melting when the weather turns warm.

Thinking Skills — divergent thinking; fluency; following directions   *Number of students at this center* — up to 4

Name _____

Building a Snowman

1. Fold your drawing paper into eight boxes.
   List or draw ways to make a snowman.

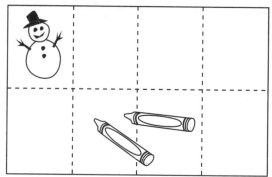

2. Draw or write to show how you would keep a snowman frozen.

My Snowman

88   Hands-On Thinking Activities • EMC 789

Thinking Skills — divergent thinking; fluency; following directions   Number of students at this center — up to 4

fold

Building a Snowman

Name the Snowmen

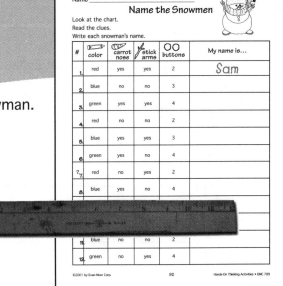

Name _____

Name the Snowmen

Look at the chart.
Read the clues.
Write each snowman's name.

#	color	carrot nose	stick arms	OO buttons	My name is...
1.	red	yes	yes	2	Sam
2.	blue	no	no	3	
3.	green	yes	yes	4	
4.	red	no	no	2	
5.	blue	yes	yes	3	
6.	green	yes	no	4	
7.	red	no	yes	2	
8.	blue	yes	no	4	
11.	blue	no	no	2	
12.	green	no	yes	4	

©2001 by Evan-Moor Corp.   92   Hands-On Thinking Activities • EMC 789

Student Task

Students read clues to help them name each snowman.

Materials

- pages 93–97 for center chart
- colored tagboard
- pencils
- rulers
- cup of counters
- page 92, reproduced for each student
- center sign on page 99

Steps to Follow

1. Prepare materials needed for the center.

   Glue the snowmen on pages 93–97 to a sheet of colored tagboard. Place the chart on the center table.

2. Students use the clues on the record sheet to identify each snowman. They then write the snowman's name on the record sheet.

   Demonstrate how to use a ruler placed under each line of clues to help students keep their place as they read the clues.

   Students may place a counter on each snowman on the chart as it is identified.

3. Extend the activity by asking students to draw a snowman on the back of their record sheets and then write clues describing it.

Thinking Skills — classifying; ordering; observing; following directions   **Number of students at this center** — up to 4

Name _____

Name the Snowmen

Look at the chart.
Read the clues.
Write each snowman's name.

#	color	carrot nose	stick arms	buttons	My name is...
1.	red	yes	yes	2	Sam
2.	blue	no	no	3	
3.	green	yes	yes	4	
4.	red	no	no	2	
5.	blue	yes	yes	3	
6.	green	yes	no	4	
7.	red	no	yes	2	
8.	blue	yes	no	4	
9.	green	no	yes	3	
10.	red	yes	no	3	
11.	blue	no	no	2	
12.	green	no	yes	4	

Sam

Jim

Tony

Bob

Hands-On Thinking Activities • EMC 789

Hands-On Thinking Activities • EMC 789

Raul

Lee

Pete

Jose

Hands-On Thinking Activities • EMC 789

96

97

Hands-On Thinking Activities • EMC 789

fold

Name the Snowmen

Spring Activity Centers

Thinking Skills Assessed

Name of Center	Following Directions	Classifying	Sorting	Observing	Generalizing	Ordering	Divergent Thinking	Comparing/ Contrasting	Fluency	Deductive Reasoning	Mental Imagery
Spring Flowers	✿	✿				✿					
Rabbit and Hen	✿							✿			
What Do You Hear?	✿	✿	✿								
Find the Flower	✿	✿		✿		✿					
Carrot Nibbles	✿			✿							
May Baskets	✿				✿						
Building a Birdhouse	✿					✿					
A Bird's-Eye View	✿										✿
How Does Your Garden Grow?	✿									✿	
A Spring Bouquet	✿						✿		✿		

Name _____

Spring

Color the flowers.

Make each flower different in one way.

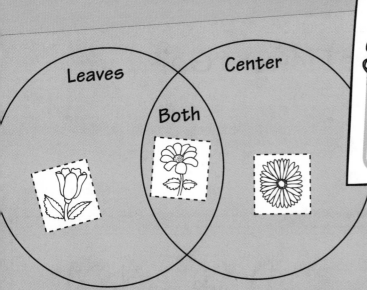

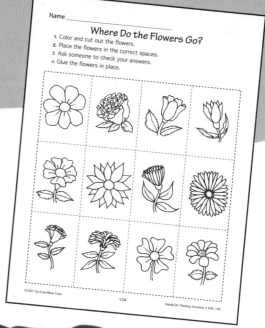

Student Task

Students color and cut out flowers, sort them, and place them on a Venn diagram in the correct categories.

Materials

- 12″ x 18″ (30.5 x 45.5 cm) construction paper, one per student
- black marking pen
- scissors and glue
- page 104, reproduced for each student
- center sign on page 105

Steps to Follow

1. Prepare materials needed for the center.

   Make a Venn diagram for each student by drawing large circles on the construction paper sheets. Label the spaces as shown. (This is a great job for parent volunteers.)

2. Introduce the center by reviewing how to use a Venn diagram. Be sure students are clear about the attributes they are looking for.

3. Students color and cut out the flowers, sort them, and place them on the Venn diagram in the correct categories.

   Have students ask someone to check their answers before gluing down the flowers.

4. Extend the activity for more able students by asking them to list other attributes of the flowers on the back of their diagram sheets.

Thinking Skills — classifying; ordering; following directions   **Number of students at this center** — up to 4

Name _____

Where Do the Flowers Go?

1. Color and cut out the flowers.
2. Place the flowers in the correct spaces.
3. Ask someone to check your answers.
4. Glue the flowers in place.

Thinking Skills — classifying; ordering; following directions   Number of students at this center — up to 4

fold

Spring Flowers

Hands-On Thinking Activities • EMC 789

Student Task

Students cut out cards containing facts about a rabbit and a hen. They then sort the cards and place them in the correct categories.

Materials

- 9″ x 12″ (23 x 30.5 cm) construction paper, one per student
- scissors
- glue
- page 108, reproduced for each student
- center sign on page 109

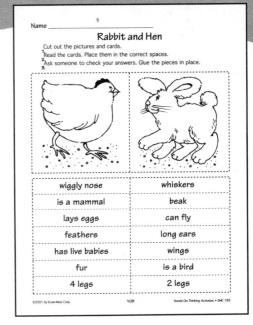

Steps to Follow

1. Prepare materials needed for the center.

2. Introduce the center. Show students how to fold the construction paper in half the long way.

   Explain that they are to cut out the pictures and glue one at the top of each column. They then cut out the phrase cards and place them in the correct boxes on the construction paper.

   Have students ask someone to check their answers before gluing down the cards.

3. Extend the activity for more able students by asking them to list on the back of their diagram sheets other ways the rabbit and hen are alike or different.

Thinking Skills — comparing and contrasting; following directions   **Number of students at this center** — up to 4

Name _____

Rabbit and Hen

1. Cut out the pictures and cards.

2. Read the cards. Place them in the correct spaces.

3. Ask someone to check your answers. Glue the pieces in place.

wiggly nose	whiskers
is a mammal	beak
lays eggs	can fly
feathers	long ears
has live babies	wings
fur	is a bird
4 legs	2 legs

fold

Rabbit and Hen

Hands-On Thinking Activities • EMC 789

Student Task

Students use their sense of hearing to classify items by sound.

Materials

- 16 plastic eggs
- items to fill eggs: pennies, marbles, raisins, rice, small jelly beans, marshmallows, safety pins, toothpicks
- permanent marking pen
- tape
- a basket to hold the eggs
- page 112, reproduced for each student
- center sign on page 113

Steps to Follow

1. Prepare materials needed for the center.

Number the eggs from 1 to 16 with a permanent pen. Fill each egg with just a few objects so that you can hear them rattle. Glue them tightly shut. When the glue is dry, tape the seam securely.

Be sure to keep an answer key so YOU will know which eggs contain which objects.

2. Students shake the eggs, listening carefully to the sound made by the objects inside. When they have found two eggs that match, they write the numbers on their record sheets.

3. Extend the activity by asking students to try to identify the objects making the sound in the eggs.

Thinking Skills — sorting; classifying; following directions   **Number of students at this center** — up to 4

Name _____

What Do You Hear?

Shake the eggs and listen to the sound.

Match two eggs with the same sound.

Write their numbers next to the item you think is in both eggs.

pennies (____) and (____)

marbles (____) and (____)

raisins (____) and (____)

jelly beans (____) and (____)

marshmallows (____) and (____)

safety pins (____) and (____)

rice (____) and (____)

toothpicks (____) and (____)

Thinking Skills — sorting; classifying; following directions   **Number of students at this center —** up to 4

fold

What Do You Hear?

Student Task

Students read clues to help them find the number of each flower.

Materials

- pages 117–121 for center chart
- colored tagboard
- pencils
- rulers
- cup of counters
- page 116, reproduced for each student
- center sign on page 123

Steps to Follow

1. Prepare materials needed for the center.

Glue the flowers on pages 117–121 to a sheet of colored tagboard. Place the chart on the center table.

2. Students use the clues on the record sheet to identify each flower. They then write the flower's number on the record sheet.

Demonstrate how to use a ruler placed under each line of clues to help students keep their place as they read the clues.

Students can place a counter on each flower on the chart as it is identified.

3. Extend the activity by asking students to draw on the back of their record sheets a flower and then write clues describing it.

Thinking Skills — classifying; ordering; observing; following directions   **Number of students at this center** — up to 4

Name _____

Find the Flower

Look at the chart.
Read the clues.
Write each flower's number.

#	color	petals	black center	leaves	My number is...
1.	blue	4	no	0	5
2.	red	3	no	2	
3.	orange	5	no	2	
4.	red	5	yes	0	
5.	red	5	no	1	
6.	orange	4	yes	2	
7.	blue	3	no	2	
8.	orange	5	yes	1	
9.	red	4	no	0	
10.	blue	3	yes	1	
11.	orange	5	yes	0	
12.	blue	4	no	1	

117

121

Hands-On Thinking Activities • EMC 789

Thinking Skills — classifying; ordering; observing; following directions   Number of students at this center — up to 4

fold

Find the Flower

Hands-On Thinking Activities • EMC 789

orange smooth
hard rough
long small
pointy tasty
crunchy damp
dry

Carrot Nibbles— Using My Five Senses

Name _____
Using My Five Senses

How my carrot looks
How my carrot smells
How my carrot tastes
How my carrot sounds
How my carrot feels

©2001 by Evan-Moor Corp.   126   Hands-On Thinking Activities • EMC 789

Student Task

Students experience a carrot with all of their senses. They write words or phrases on a record sheet to describe what they sense.

Materials

- carrot pieces
- small paper plates
- pencils or crayons
- chart paper
- page 126, reproduced for each student
- center sign on page 127

Steps to Follow

1. Prepare materials needed for the center.

   At the beginning of each center session, place several carrot pieces on a small paper plate for each student at the center.

2. Introduce the center. Brainstorm a list of words that describe how things taste, sound, feel, smell, and look. Write these words on a chart to serve as a word bank at the center. (Or use the chart started on page 11.)

3. Encourage students at the center to talk about what they discover as they taste, feel, etc., their carrots. Then they write descriptive words in each section of the worksheet.

Thinking Skills — observing; following directions   **Number of students at this center** — up to 4

Name _____

Using My Five Senses

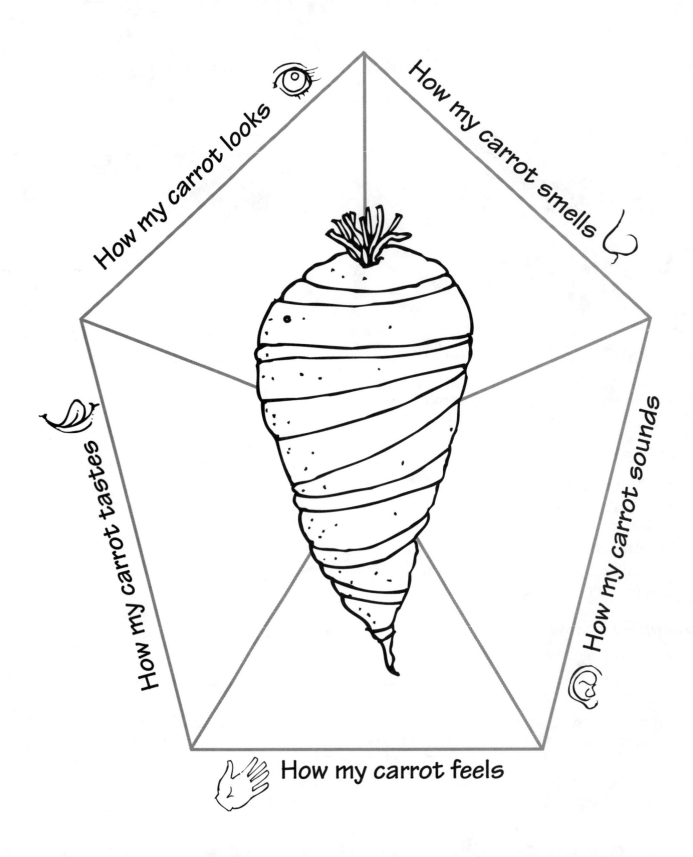

How my carrot looks

How my carrot smells

How my carrot tastes

How my carrot sounds

How my carrot feels

Thinking Skills — observing; following directions   **Number of students at this center** — up to 4

fold

Carrot Nibbles— Using My Five Senses

127   *Hands-On Thinking Activities • EMC 789*

Hands-On Thinking Activities • EMC 789

Student Task

Students generalize what characteristics are common to a set of flowers.

Materials

- pencils
- page 130, reproduced for each student
- center sign on page 131

Steps to Follow

1. Prepare materials needed for the center.

2. Review ways to solve this type of puzzle. Remind students to look carefully at the pictures and to ask themselves questions such as, "What is the same about the pictures in row one? How are the pictures in row one different?"

3. Students look for the characteristics shared by the flowers in row one but not found on the flowers in row two. They then draw a flower that may go into the May basket.

Thinking Skills — generalizing; following directions   **Number of students at this center** — up to 4

May Baskets

These flowers may go in my May basket.

These flowers may not go in my May basket.

Draw a flower that may go in the May basket.

Note: Place this sign on the table to identify the center.

Thinking Skills — generalizing; following directions   Number of students at this center — up to 4

fold

May Baskets

Building a Birdhouse

Name _____

Building a Birdhouse

Cut the pictures apart. Paste them in order.

How was the birdhouse used?

©2001 by Evan-Moor Corp. 134 Hands-On Thinking Activities • EMC 789

Student Task

Students place in order the steps for making a birdhouse. They then draw a picture to show how the finished birdhouse is used.

Materials

- 4″ x 18″ (10 x 45.5 cm) construction paper strips, one per student
- writing paper
- scissors and glue
- pencils, crayons
- page 134, reproduced for each student
- center sign on page 135

Steps to Follow

1. Prepare materials needed for the center.

2. Introduce the center. Explain to students that they are to cut the pieces apart and then paste them in order on their construction paper strip. Remind them to start with the lumber and tools on the left side of the strip. In the blank box, they are to draw a picture showing how the finished birdhouse is used. This will be the last picture in the sequence.

3. Extend the activity by asking students to write about each step on a sheet of writing paper.

Thinking Skills — ordering; following directions   **Number of students at this center** — up to 4

Name _____

Building a Birdhouse

Cut the pictures apart. Paste them in order.

How was the
birdhouse used?

Note: Place this sign on the table to identify the center.

Thinking Skills — ordering; following directions   **Number of students at this center** — up to 4

fold

Building a Birdhouse

135

Hands-On Thinking Activities • EMC 789

Student Task

Students match a bird's-eye view of playground equipment with the ground-level view.

Materials

- pencils
- crayons
- page 138, reproduced for each student
- center sign on page 139

Steps to Follow

1. Prepare materials needed for the center.
2. Introduce the center. Have students take a few minutes to observe common items in the classroom from above (chair, table, plant, etc.). Have them describe the items.
3. Using page 138, students match the two views of each item. Extend the activity by having students draw on the back of page 138 their own bird's-eye view of a common item.

Thinking Skills — mental imagery; following directions   **Number of students at this center** — up to 4

A Bird's-Eye View

Pretend you are a bird flying over the playground.
Match the bird's-eye view with each piece of equipment.

Thinking Skills — mental imagery; following directions   **Number of students at this center** — up to 4

fold

A Bird's-Eye View

Hands-On Thinking Activities • EMC 789

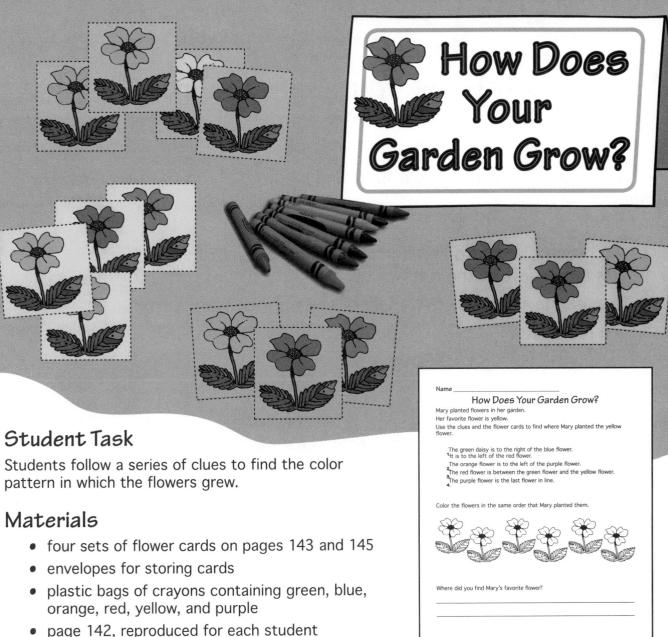

Student Task

Students follow a series of clues to find the color pattern in which the flowers grew.

Materials

- four sets of flower cards on pages 143 and 145
- envelopes for storing cards
- plastic bags of crayons containing green, blue, orange, red, yellow, and purple
- page 142, reproduced for each student
- center sign on page 147

Steps to Follow

1. Prepare materials needed for the center.

   Laminate and cut out the four sets of flower cards. Store each set in its own envelope. Students must replace the cards in the correct envelopes after finishing the activity.

2. Introduce the center. Review strategies for solving this type of puzzle. Model how to place the cards to the right and left of each other as called for in the clues.

3. Students read the clues and move the flower cards around to determine where Mary's favorite flower is growing. When they are satisfied that the flower cards are in the correct order, students record the order by coloring the flowers on their record sheets.

4. Extend the activity by having students develop their own flower garden puzzle on a sheet of drawing paper.

Thinking Skills — deductive reasoning; following directions   **Number of students at this center** — up to 4

Name _____

How Does Your Garden Grow?

Mary planted flowers in her garden.

Her favorite flower is yellow.

Use the clues and the flower cards to find where Mary planted the yellow flower.

1. The green daisy is to the right of the blue flower.
    It is to the left of the red flower.
2. The orange flower is to the left of the purple flower.
3. The red flower is between the green flower and the yellow flower.
4. The purple flower is the last flower in line.

Color the flowers in the same order that Mary planted them.

Where did you find Mary's favorite flower?

_____

_____

Hands-On Thinking Activities • EMC 789

Hands-On Thinking Activities • EMC 789

Hands-On Thinking Activities • EMC 789

Hands-On Thinking Activities • EMC 789

Thinking Skills — deductive reasoning; following directions   Number of students at this center — up to 4

fold

How Does Your Garden Grow?

Hands-On Thinking Activities • EMC 789

Student Task

Students think of containers in which to carry a bouquet of flowers. They then explain which container they would use if giving a bouquet of flowers to someone special.

Materials

- pencils
- page 150, reproduced for each student
- center sign on page 151

Steps to Follow

1. Prepare materials needed for the center.

2. Students pretend they have picked a bunch of flowers. They then think of six ways to carry the flowers. They draw or label their suggestions.

3. Students then select one of the containers and on the back of their worksheet explain why they would use it to give the bouquet of flowers to someone special.

Thinking Skills — divergent thinking; fluency; following directions   *Number of students at this center* — up to 4

Name _____

A Spring Bouquet

I picked a bunch of flowers.
Draw or name six things I can put them in.

1.	2.	3.
4.	5.	6.

I am going to give these flowers to someone.

Draw the best container to use.

Tell why you used it.

Note: Place this sign on the table to identify the center.

Thinking Skills — divergent thinking; fluency; following directions   Number of students at this center — up to 4

fold

A Spring Bouquet

Hands-On Thinking Activities • EMC 789

Hands-On Thinking Activities • EMC 789

Summer Activity Centers

Thinking Skills Assessed

Name of Center	Following Directions	Classifying	Sorting	Observing	Generalizing	Ordering	Divergent Thinking	Comparing/ Contrasting	Fluency	Deductive Reasoning	Mental Imagery
Clara's Closet	🍂	🍂	🍂								
Lemonade	🍂			🍂							
Speedster	🍂				🍂						
Let's Skate	🍂							🍂			
I Scream for Ice Cream	🍂	🍂		🍂		🍂					
At the Zoo	🍂									🍂	
Getting Down the Slide	🍂						🍂		🍂		
Cookie Jar	🍂	🍂				🍂					

Name _____

Summer

Color the ice-cream sundaes.
Make each sundae different in one way.

Student Task

Students organize into categories the items that go in Clara's closet.

Materials

- scissors
- glue
- pencils
- page 156, reproduced for each student
- center sign on page 157

Steps to Follow

1. Prepare the materials needed for the center.

2. Students cut out the items, decide what goes together, and then place the items in the closet.

   Before gluing down the pieces, students explain to someone what they have put together and the rule they followed.

3. Students draw one more appropriate item in each section of the closet.

4. Extend the activity by asking students to think of a second way the items might be organized. They may draw or list their ideas on the back of the record sheet.

Thinking Skills — classifying; sorting; following directions   **Number of students at this center** — up to 4

Name _____

Clara's Closet

Clara's closet was a mess.

Help her organize things.

Then paste them neatly in the closet.

Tell someone what rule you used to organize things.

Draw one more thing in each part of the closet.

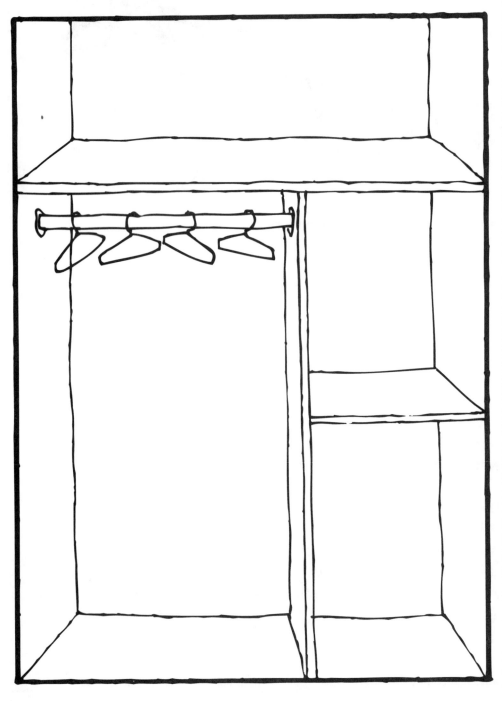

Thinking Skills — classifying; sorting; following directions   Number of students at this center — up to 4

fold

Clara's Closet

Hands-On Thinking Activities • EMC 789

Hands-On Thinking Activities • EMC 789

sweet   tasty
sour   lemony
wet   cold
pink   sugary
yellow
refreshing

Lemonade—
Using My
Five Senses

Student Task

Students experience lemonade with all of their senses. They write words or phrases on a record sheet to describe what they sense.

Materials

- plastic cups
- lemonade, regular and pink
- pencils or crayons
- page 160, reproduced for each student
- center sign on page 161

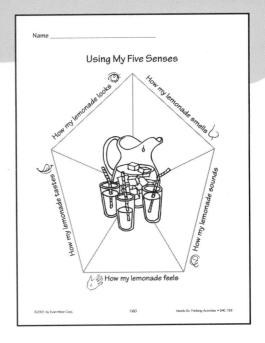

Steps to Follow

1. Prepare materials needed for the center.

   At the beginning of each center session, pour cups of lemonade for the students to observe. Use regular and pink lemonade to encourage more variety in the students' descriptions.

2. Introduce the center. Brainstorm a list of words that describe how things taste, sound, feel, smell, and look. Write these words on a chart to serve as a word bank at the center. (Or use the chart started on page 11.)

3. Encourage students at the center to talk about what they discover as they taste, feel, etc., their lemonade. Then they write descriptive words in each part of the worksheet.

Thinking Skills — observing; following directions   **Number of students at this center** — up to 4

Name _____

Using My Five Senses

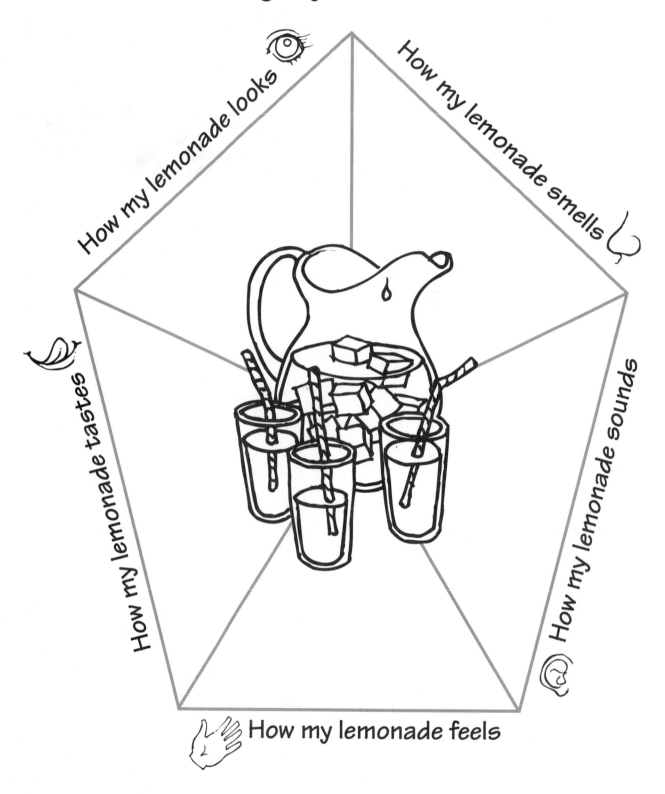

How my lemonade looks

How my lemonade smells

How my lemonade tastes

How my lemonade sounds

How my lemonade feels

Thinking Skills — observing; following directions   Number of students at this center — up to 4

fold

Lemonade—
Using My Five Senses

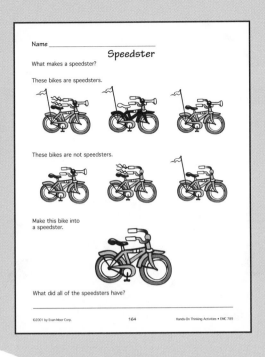

Student Task

Students generalize what characteristics are common to a set of bicycles.

Materials

- pencils
- page 164, reproduced for each student
- center sign on page 165

Steps to Follow

1. Prepare materials needed for the center.

2. Review ways to solve this type of puzzle. Remind students to look carefully at the pictures and to ask themselves questions such as, "What is the same about the pictures in row one? How are the pictures in row one different?"

3. Students look for the characteristics shared by the bikes in row one but not found on the bikes in row two. They then add details to the final bike to turn it into a speedster.

Thinking Skills — generalizing; following directions   **Number of students at this center** — up to 4

Speedster

What makes a speedster?

These bikes are speedsters.

These bikes are not speedsters.

Make this bike into
a speedster.

What did all of the speedsters have?

_____

     Hands-On Thinking Activities • EMC 789

Thinking Skills — generalizing; following directions   **Number of students at this center** — up to 4

fold

Speedster

Hands-On Thinking Activities • EMC 789

Student Task

Students find the differences between two pairs of roller blades.

Materials

- pencils or crayons
- page 168, reproduced for each student
- center sign on page 169

Steps to Follow

1. Prepare materials needed for the center.

2. Introduce the center. Explain that there are eight ways in which the roller blades are different. Students are to list the eight ways. Encourage students to try to find the ways independently. Then, if they are having difficulty, work with the other students at the center.

3. Extend the activity by having students list ways the roller blades are alike on the back of their papers.

Thinking Skills — comparing and contrasting; following directions   **Number of students at this center** — up to 4

Name _____

Let's Skate

Look at the roller blades carefully.
Find 8 ways they are different.

1. _____

2. _____

3. _____

4. _____

5. _____

6. _____

7. _____

8. _____

Thinking Skills — comparing and contrasting; following directions   **Number of students at this center** — up to 4

fold

Let's Skate

         Hands-On Thinking Activities • EMC 789

Hands-On Thinking Activities • EMC 789

Student Task

Students read the clues to help them find the number of each ice-cream cone.

Materials

- pages 173–177 for center chart
- colored tagboard
- pencils
- rulers
- cup of counters
- page 172, reproduced for each student
- center sign on page 179

Name _____

I Scream for Ice Cream

Look at the chart.
Read the clues. Write the ice-cream cone's number.

#	flat bottom	ice-cream flavor	scoops	lines on cone	I am number...
1.	yes	chocolate	3	yes	7
2.	no	chocolate	1	yes	
3.	yes	strawberry	1	no	
4.	no	strawberry	2	no	
5.	no	vanilla	1	yes	
8.	no	chocolate	3	no	
9.	yes	vanilla	1	yes	
10.	yes	chocolate	2	yes	
11.	no	strawberry	2	yes	
12.	no	vanilla	2	yes	

©2001 by Evan-Moor Corp. 172 Hands-On Thinking Activities • EMC 789

Steps to Follow

1. Prepare materials needed for the center.

   Glue the ice-cream cones on pages 173–177 to a sheet of colored tagboard. Place the chart on the center table.

2. Students use the clues on the record sheet to identify each ice-cream cone. They write the cone's number on the record sheet.

   Demonstrate how to use a ruler placed under each line of clues to help students keep their place as they read the clues.

   Students may place a counter on each ice-cream cone on the chart as it is identified.

3. Extend the activity by asking students to draw an ice-cream cone on the back of their record sheets and then write clues describing it.

Thinking Skills — classifying; ordering; observing; following directions   **Number of students at this center** — up to 4

Name _____

I Scream for Ice Cream

Look at the chart.

Read the clues. Write the ice-cream cone's number.

#	flat bottom	ice-cream flavor	scoops	lines on cone	I am number...
1.	yes	chocolate	3	yes	7
2.	no	chocolate	1	yes	
3.	yes	strawberry	1	no	
4.	no	strawberry	2	no	
5.	no	vanilla	1	yes	
6.	yes	strawberry	2	yes	
7.	yes	vanilla	3	no	
8.	no	chocolate	3	no	
9.	yes	vanilla	1	yes	
10.	yes	chocolate	2	yes	
11.	no	strawberry	2	yes	
12.	no	vanilla	2	yes	

Hands-On Thinking Activities • EMC 789

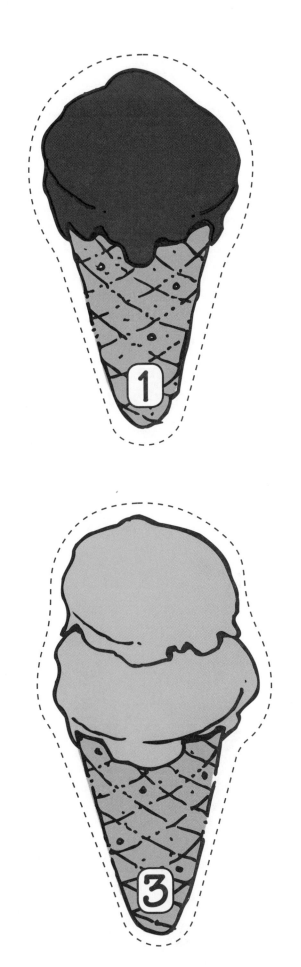

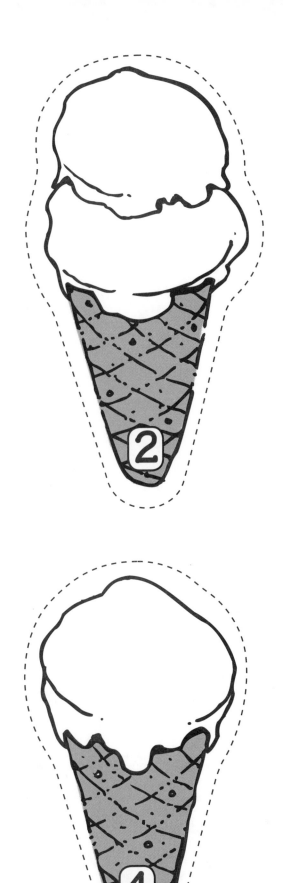

Hands-On Thinking Activities • EMC 789

Hands-On Thinking Activities • EMC 789

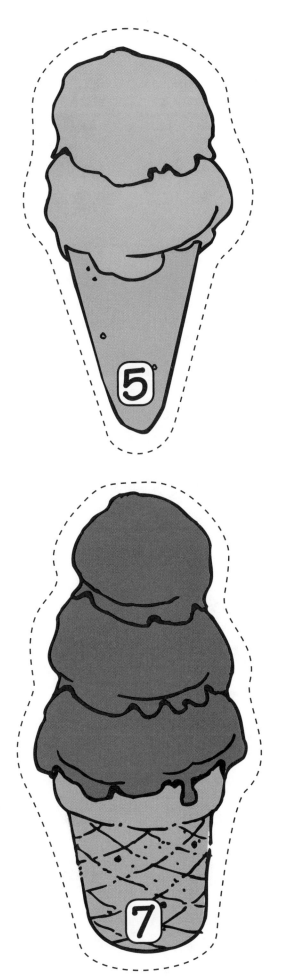

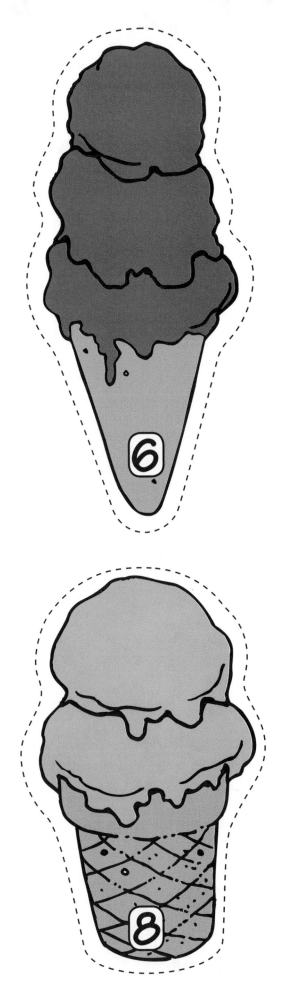

Hands-On Thinking Activities • EMC 789

Hands-On Thinking Activities • EMC 789

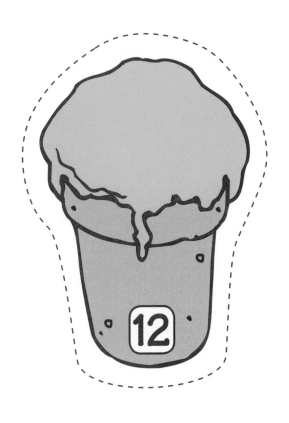

Hands-On Thinking Activities • EMC 789

Hands-On Thinking Activities • EMC 789

fold

Thinking Skills — classifying; ordering; observing; following directions   **Number of students at this center** — up to 4

I Scream for Ice Cream

Hands-On Thinking Activities • EMC 789

Student Task

Students use clues to figure out which zoo animal each family member liked best.

Materials

- container of counters
- crayons
- page 182, reproduced for each student
- center sign on page 183

Steps to Follow

1. Prepare materials needed for the center.

2. Discuss strategies for working a matrix. Read the clues and put a counter on the correct box. If there can be no other answer for that person, make an X in all the other boxes after that name. Since each person chose only one animal as their favorite, make an X on all the other boxes under that animal. For example: Mark liked the elephant, so put a counter on elephant in Mark's row. Make an X on all the other animals in Mark's row. Also make an X on all the other boxes under elephant.

   Explain to students that once they are happy with their answers, they are to remove the counters one at a time, coloring in the boxes they have marked.

   If students have had limited experience solving a matrix problem, have them work in pairs.

Thinking Skills — deductive reasoning; following directions   **Number of students at this center** — up to 4

Name _____

At the Zoo

The Smith family went to the zoo.
Use the clues to find out which animal each family member liked best.
Color the correct boxes.

1. Mother liked the animal that nibbled leaves off a tall tree.

2. Father liked the animal that hung from the branch of a tree.

3. Mark liked the heaviest animal best.

4. Which animal did Monica like best? _____

Father				
Monica				
Mother				
Mark				

Thinking Skills — deductive reasoning; following directions   **Number of students at this center** — up to 4

fold

At the Zoo

Hands-On Thinking Activities • EMC 789

Student Task

Students think of three ways to get down from a slide. They then write about which way they would use to get a frightened child off the slide.

Materials

- writing paper
- pencils and crayons
- page 186, reproduced for each student
- center sign on page 187

Steps to Follow

1. Prepare materials needed for the center.
2. Students think of three ways to get down from a slide. They draw or write their suggestions.
3. They then select the way they think would be best to help a frightened child get down the slide, and write about it on a separate piece of paper.

Thinking Skills — divergent thinking; following directions; fluency   **Number of students at this center** — up to 4

Getting Down the Slide

Think of three ways to get down from a slide.
Draw or write about one way in each box.

This little child is afraid to come down the slide.

Which way would you help get him down?

Why would you use that way?

Write your answer on a sheet of paper.

Thinking Skills — divergent thinking; following directions; fluency   **Number of students at this center** — up to 4

fold

Getting Down the Slide

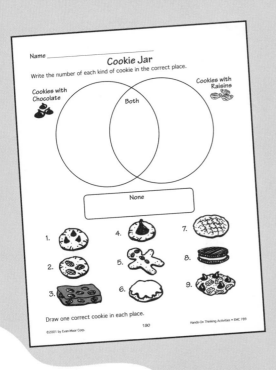

Student Task

Students categorize cookies on a Venn diagram.

Materials

- pencils
- page 190, reproduced for each student
- center sign on page 191

Steps to Follow

1. Prepare materials needed for the center.

2. Introduce the center by reviewing how to use a Venn diagram. Be sure students are clear about the attributes they are looking for. Model how they are to write the numbers of their answers in the spaces.

3. Extend the activity for more able students by asking them to list on the back of their diagram sheets other attributes of the cookies.

Thinking Skills — classifying; ordering; following directions   **Number of students at this center** — up to 4

Name _____

Cookie Jar

Write the number of each kind of cookie in the correct place.

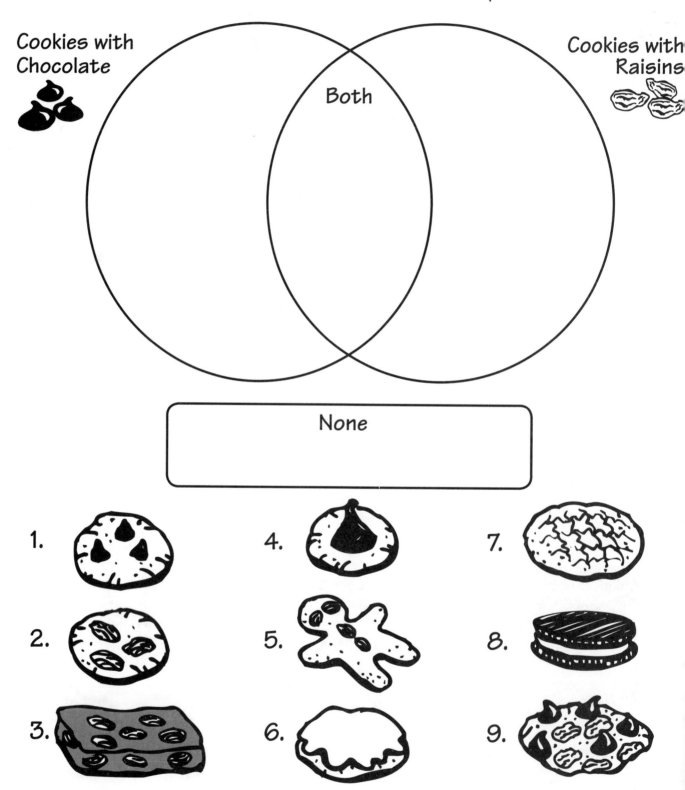

Cookies with Chocolate

Cookies with Raisins

Both

None

1.

2.

3.

4.

5.

6.

7.

8.

9.

Draw one correct cookie in each place.

Hands-On Thinking Activities • EMC 789

Thinking Skills — classifying; ordering; following directions   Number of students at this center — up to 4

fold

Cookie Jar

HAVE A COOKIE

Answer Key

page 24

Name the Scarecrows
1. Look at the chart.
2. Read the clues.
3. Write each scarecrow's name.

#	color	scarf	hat	gloves	crow	My name is...
1.	blue	no	yes	yes	yes	Jake
2.	purple	yes	yes	yes	no	Ted
3.	green	no	yes	no	no	Jon
4.	orange	yes	yes	no	no	Jose
5.	orange	yes	no	no	yes	Will
6.	blue	yes	yes	no	no	George
7.	green	no	yes	no	yes	Hank
8.	purple	no	yes	yes	no	Lee
9.	blue	no	no	yes	yes	Herbie
10.	orange	no	no	yes	no	Arnold
11.	purple	no	yes	yes	no	Carlos
12.	green	no	no	yes	no	Kai

page 40

Larry's Leaves
Help Larry pick leaves for his collection.
These are Larry's leaves.

These are not Larry's leaves.

Mark the leaves that Larry would pick for his collection.

What did all of Larry's leaves have?
5 veins (lines) and a long stem

page 48

Who Likes Pumpkin Pie?
Use the clues to find out what each child had for a snack.
Color the correct boxes.

1. Tomas put salt on his snack.
2. Ann held a cone to eat her snack.
3. Bill and Kim ate their snacks with a fork.
4. Bill doesn't like cake.

	pumpkin pie	ice cream	popcorn	cake
Ann	X	■	X	X
Bill	■	X	X	X
Kim	X	X	X	■
Tomas	X	X	■	X

Turn this paper over. Draw a snack you like to eat. Tell why you like it.

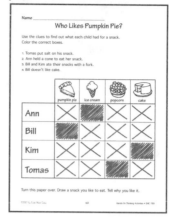

page 72

Polar Bears
Look at the polar bears.
How are they alike?
How are they different?

Mark the two bears that are just alike.

page 80

A Herd of Reindeer
Reindeer live in herds.

These reindeer are a part of a herd.

These reindeer are not a part of the herd.

Make this reindeer a part of the herd.

What rule did you follow?
Reindeer with both antlers and a colored nose are part of the herd.

page 84

Who Likes Hot Chocolate?
Use the clues to find out what each child had to drink.
Color the correct boxes.

1. Peggy and Jake drink fruit juice.
2. Jake's drink is made from oranges.
3. Sal's drink comes from a cow.
4. Maddy's drink is hot.

	hot chocolate	orange juice	milk	apple juice
Sal	X	X	■	X
Peggy	X	X	X	■
Maddy	■	X	X	X
Jake	X	■	X	X

page 92

Name the Snowmen
Look at the chart.
Read the clues.
Write each snowman's name.

#	color	carrot nose	stick arms	buttons	My name is...
1.	red	yes	no	2	Sam
2.	blue	no	no	3	Bob
3.	green	yes	no	4	Ned
4.	red	no	no	2	Jose
5.	blue	yes	yes	3	Tony
6.	green	yes	no	4	Lee
7.	red	no	yes	2	Pete
8.	blue	no	no	4	Ken
9.	blue	no	yes	3	Raul
10.	red	yes	no	3	Jim
11.	blue	no	no	2	Tom
12.	green	no	yes	4	Carl

page 108

Rabbit and Hen
1. Cut out the pictures and cards.
2. Read the cards. Place them in the correct spaces.
3. Ask someone to check your answers. Glue the pieces in place.

wiggly nose	R	whiskers	R
is a mammal	R	beak	H
lays eggs	H	can fly	H
feathers	H	long ears	R
has live babies	R	wings	H
fur	R	is a bird	H
4 legs	R	2 legs	H

page 116

Find the Flower
Look at the chart.
Read the clues.
Write each flower's number.

#	color	petals	black center	leaves	My number is...
1.	blue	4	no	0	5
2.	red	3	no	2	1
3.	orange	5	no	2	9
4.	red	5	yes	0	4
5.	red	5	no	1	7
6.	orange	4	yes	2	6
7.	blue	3	no	2	8
8.	orange	5	yes	1	3
9.	red	4	no	0	10
10.	blue	3	yes	1	11
11.	orange	5	yes	0	12
12.	blue	4	no	1	2

page 130

May Baskets
These flowers may go in my May basket.

These flowers may not go in my May basket.

Draw a flower that may go in the May Basket.

flower must have a long stem and leaves

page 142

How Does Your Garden Grow?
Mary planted flowers in her garden.
Her favorite flower is yellow.
Use the clues and the flower cards to find where Mary planted the yellow flower.

1. The green daisy is to the right of the blue flower.
   It is to the left of the red flower.
2. The orange flower is to the left of the purple flower.
3. The red flower is between the green flower and the yellow flower.
4. The purple flower is the last flower in line.

Color the flowers in the same order that Mary planted them.

blue   green   red   yellow   orange   purple

Where did you find Mary's favorite flower?
The yellow flower is between the red and the orange flowers.

page 164

Speedster
What makes a speedster?

These bikes are speedsters.

These bikes are not speedsters.

Make this bike into a speedster.

What did all of the speedsters have?
All speedsters have a flag and a horn.

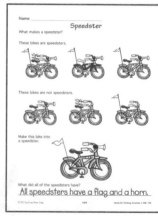

page 168

Let's Skate
Look at the roller blades carefully.
Find 8 ways they are different.

1. one has stripes on the side; the other is black
2. one has stripes inside; the other is white inside
3. one has white toes; the other has black toes
4. one pair has stars; the other has circles
5. the wheels are different colors
6. one pair has zippers; the other has laces
7. one pair has arrows on the blades; the other has wavy lines
8. one has a B, the other has an A

page 172

I Scream for Ice Cream
Look at the chart.
Read the clues. Write the ice-cream cone's number.

#	flat bottom	ice-cream flavor	scoops	lines on cone	I am number...
1.	yes	chocolate	3	yes	7
2.	no	chocolate	1	yes	1
3.	yes	strawberry	1	no	12
4.	no	strawberry	2	no	5
5.	no	vanilla	1	yes	4
6.	no	strawberry	2	yes	8
7.	yes	vanilla	3	no	11
8.	no	chocolate	3	no	6
9.	yes	vanilla	1	yes	9
10.	yes	chocolate	2	yes	10
11.	no	strawberry	2	yes	3
12.	no	vanilla	2	yes	2

page 182

At the Zoo
The Smith family went to the zoo.
Use the clues to find out which animal each family member liked best.
Color the correct boxes.

1. Mother liked the animal that nibbled leaves off a tall tree.
2. Father liked the animal that hung from the branch of a tree.
3. Mark liked the heaviest animal best.
4. Which animal did Monica like best? lion

	elephant	giraffe	monkey	lion
Father	X	X	■	X
Monica	X	X	X	■
Mother	X	■	X	X
Mark	■	X	X	X

page 190

Cookie Jar
Write the number of each kind of cookie in the correct place.

Cookies with Chocolate   Cookies with Raisins

Both

| 1 4 8 | 9 3 | 2 5 |

None

6   7

Draw one correct cookie in each place.

1.   4.   7.
2.   5.   8.
3.   6.   9.

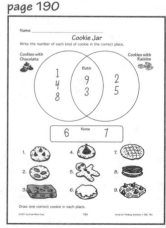

Hands-On Thinking Activities • EMC 789